I Love You You Little Sh!t

An essential, 12-step program for dealing with your bratty-ass teen and living the life you were meant to live before they grew up and began crushing your soul!

KAT and STEWART

Copyright © 2023 by Kat and Stewart

All rights reserved. This book or any portion thereof may not be reproduced or used in

any manner whatsoever without the express written permission of the publisher except

for the use of brief quotations in a book review.

Publishing Services provided by Paper Raven Books LLC

Printed in the United States of America

First Printing, 2023

Paperback ISBN: 979-8-9894978-1-2

Disclaimer:

Our attorneys, who we think are overly cautious but super cool, are making us tell you that these books are based on our personal histories and remedies that we discovered for ourselves and not psychological or medical advice for you, the reader.

I mean, we think we got this shit pretty well dialed in and we're crushing it right now, but hey… you do you. Legally.

Do you know the allegory of...

The swimmer and the pool?

The parents are the pool.
The water is life, experiences, etc.
The swimmer is your teenage daughter.

Your daughter swims in the water with her friends, splashing, diving, doing tricks, and never giving any thought to how the water stays in one place and is kept stable by the pool.

But at some point, she gets held underwater, splashed too much, and she needs a break, so she swims to the side and hangs on. For a moment, you might be thinking "She's back!"

But inevitably she gets her breath back and heads back into the water, dashing the parents' hopes that perhaps she was back for good.

Note to the pool parents (paraphrased from Dr. Lisa Damour, Ph.D.):

Teen girls mature faster than boys do. When they are young, they see what they are going to become and realize early on that they need to be ready. At some point, they unconsciously decide that they are no longer the little girl, they are a pre-woman. Anything that smacks of little girl-dom is wrong and must be excised immediately, putting their relationship with you off to the side, returning on an as-needed basis.

"HOW DID I GET TO THIS INSANE POINT IN MY LIFE?"

"What happened to my little girl?"

Here's what happened… puberty. You raised this sweet little angel from her first breath to her teens and it seemed like she was always going to be that perfect little girl. And then, one day, as if a light switch were turned off, she changed.

You're reading this because you have gotten to that wonderfully fucked up phase in a teen girl's life where she has turned into the monster that everyone warned you about.

"Not my little baby," you said, "How could that be? She's so perfect!" And then… The Kraken!

We put this book together for you because we have been there.

Four. Times.

We made every mistake and also sought out a lot of wisdom from experts like Dr. Damour and others. And so, we decided to create a simple, 12-step guidance program for you to get you through this unbelievably difficult time.

We made it, so can you.

Be patient and loving, follow the 12 steps of dealing with your teen terrorist, and you'll get through it.

Step 1

EMBRACE THE CHAOS.

Accept that teenage girls come with a whirlwind of emotions and drama. And the worst part of all is they feel fully justified in their position.

You like roller coasters? You'd better because this ride is nearing the top and you're about to take the plunge at high speed.

Buckle up!

Say this first part out loud:

- My fucking teenager is a hurricane in flannel pajama pants!!
- I'm not even sure they actually are my child!
- They're making me consider a career in alcoholism!

Okay, good.

MANTRA FOR STEP 1:
THIS SUCKS!

Repeat after me:

- *I'm responsible for their growth*
- *I am responsible for my reactions*
- *I have a lot of 'not reacting' to learn*

Great! That's the first step. When in doubt, if you're starting to feel like moving to a state where murdering your child is legal, repeat the first step.

Step 2

REALIZE THIS IS NORMAL. YOU ARE STILL IN CONTROL OF YOUR REACTIONS.

Yes, your child is literally the spawn of Satan right now, and it seemed to come out of nowhere. You ask yourself "Is this my fault? How can I fix this?"

You can't. This is natural and she needs to go through this time in her life. It's time to focus on you and how you react, otherwise you'll be playing whack-a-mole with her outbursts and suffering greatly for it all.

I Love You, YOU LITTLE SH!T

Let's keep the real shit going:

- This little monster is not my kid! Was she kidnapped by aliens and replaced?
- Nothing I do will help the situation. In fact, it makes it worse.
- For now, they are the emotional enemy.

MANTRA FOR STEP 2:
FUCKING. TEENAGERS.
Got it out of your system? Good.

Repeat after me:

- *As much as I hate her right now, I realize this is normal*
- *I'm not the only parent to go through this (unfortunately)*
- *I have a shit ton of work to do*
- *I love her, I love her, I fucking love that little devil*

Step 3

MAKE A DECISION TO INVEST IN SOME KIND OF THERAPY FOR HER.

Look, you're not going to help her, she doesn't want it from you. And her friends are great, but they can only make things worse. Remember, teen girls, not the best decision-makers.

Your teen can benefit from professional help. Offer it up as an opportunity to rant about everyone in private without anyone knowing.

Time for a real shift in thinking:

- I can't change my kid; I need to understand that this is not about me and no matter what I do, she's going to hate it.
- At least I can help her find an outlet in therapy, sports, something where she can get it all out.
- At this point, I'll sell my damn car if it means toning down the nightmare.

MANTRA FOR STEP 3:
SHE DOESN'T NEED ME RIGHT NOW AND THAT'S OKAY.

Repeat after me:

- *It's possible I've rested my self-esteem on raising this child. As if I don't have any worth if she doesn't like me.*
- *I really do have a shit ton of work to do.*
- *But neither of us has to be alone. I'm going to find a therapist for her—and ME—and commit to our mental health starting today.*

Step 4

STAY VIGILANT WITH SOCIALS, LINGO, AND ACCESS TO PORN.

You're still the parent, and just because she wants you out of her room (and life), doesn't mean she gets free reign on the internet.

Time for a little gut check:

- The internet and social media are like a poison pill. They feed off the endorphins they generate.
- Shit!
- Yeah, ye who giveth the phone can also taketh away. She already hates you (sorry, sometimes), and this means you're parenting.

MANTRA FOR STEP 4:
I MAY NOT WANT TO RIGHT NOW, BUT I'LL TAKE A BULLET FOR YOU.

Action items:

- Talk to other parents about their restrictions.
- Research sites and socials to figure out how to block content or at least monitor her access to it.
- Try to be stealth about it if you can. It's better and easier to catch her if she doesn't know you're spying on her.
- YES, you get to spy on her.
- Speak with a professional about how to handle issues if they come up. Don't try this without a net.

Step 5

BUILD A BUNKER TO SURVIVE THE HORMONE STORM.

Resist the urge to drink heavily or sell them on the black market. Remember, patience is a virtue (and not illegal).

Release!

In our little world, our kids have made us cry with their attitude and cruelty. I mean, like they were mean! We were literally afraid of them!

Here's our advice for handling it:

Distance yourself, meet up with friends, walk, hike, and find other activities that give you perspective. If you are a woman, you might remember a time when you were like this. Help your man understand because it's really hard for any man to truly get it.

MANTRA FOR STEP 5:
GO TO DEF-CON 5!
Make sense? Good.

Action Item:

Create new opportunities for yourself to reconnect with what you love. You've been parenting so long, you might have forgotten!

Step 6

LET THEM FIGURE THINGS OUT— ENCOURAGE THEIR INDIVIDUALITY.

Let them express themselves and explore their interests, even if it means rainbow hair or unconventional fashion choices. As long as they are respectful to you in your home, the more freedom they feel to be fully self-expressive may make a difference.

Some personal notions you might want to try:

- I love that little shit. I really do.
- I remember who she was and can envision who she will be.
- Would I want to be held back as a young person?
- Could I maybe trade her for a boy for 2 – 4 years?

MANTRA FOR STEP 6:
LET HER EXPERIENCE THIS NEW REALITY FULLY.

She's getting ready to be a woman, remember? Help her get there.

Action items:

Speak to the mature girl she's endeavoring to become. Try not to focus on how she's not behaving well.

Give her space, let her figure things out.

Allow for an eye roll now and then—it sucks, but it's normal.

Notes

Step 7

DON'T SWEAT THE SMALL STUFF

Choose your battles wisely. Some things aren't worth the emotional energy. Save it for the important stuff.

New habits require effort:

- Catch yourself every time you begin to react to her behavior. It might be you're taking it personally, and that's about you.

Your job as a parent now is not to be their hero, it's to be their pool.

MANTRA FOR STEP 7:
STAND BY, THEY'RE GOING TO NEED YOU.

Action items:

- Begin to retrain your mind to accept that you aren't her friend, you aren't her go-to right now.
- Understand it's not forever.
- These things will help you release your reactionary side and settle you for the really important moments.

Step 8

DON'T GET ON THE CRAZY TRAIN WITH THEM.

Get that emotional flack jacket on and develop a sturdy sarcasm shield. They've got nothing on you!

Remember who you were before you had kids:

We let their behavior hurt us because we want them to look up to us and appreciate the awesome parents we are.
Yeah, that ain't happening.

MANTRA FOR STEP 8:
I DON'T HAVE TO GET SUCKED IN TO THE CRAZY!
It's easy to forget that!

Action items:

- Get a book on dealing with teenagers. Dr. Damour's Tangled is a great resource!
- Remember to practice self-care. We get so wrapped up in serving our little succubus that we forget to take care of ourselves.
- Don't get caught up in responding to the mean talk. It will give her a reason hate you even more.

Step 9

MASTER THE ART OF SELECTIVE HEARING.

Fine-tune your ability to hear the important stuff and filter out the evil teen messaging and chatter.

Is it possible? Is it likely? Is it magic?

First, let's look at what's being said:

Your little princess might be doing anything from rolling her eyes to telling you she hates you or anything in between.

This happens all the time. Remember, it's normal.

MANTRA FOR STEP 9:
THEY'RE CHILDREN. THIS IS NEW FOR THEM TOO.

The goal here is to avoid listening to or hearing the actual words and do your best to address the real issue—if there is one.

Action items:

- Don't focus on the words
- Remember to enforce respect when speaking. Disrespect is a non-starter
- Attempt as best as you can to listen for what's behind the bellowing, crying, and stomping
- When in doubt, get out of the way and let them have their moment

A teenage girl is a freight train of emotion. The best thing you can do is not to try to cross the tracks while they're barreling down on you.

Step 10

RESPECT THEIR PRIVACY.

This discipline dovetails off Step 9. It's very easy to get drawn into feelings of frustration, anger, and hurt when your baby girl erupts, and you want to invade her space, demanding an apology or even trying to talk it out.

Rookie move.

MANTRA FOR STEP 10:
DISTANCE AND TIME ARE YOUR FRIENDS RIGHT NOW!

A teen's room is their sanctuary. Don't invade, especially after a blow-up. You may want to storm in because it's 'your house' and they need to respect your rules, but do you really think crossing the border into evil-town is a good strategy?

Unless they've stolen something or have a boy in there, give them the time and distance they need. They've pushed off from the side of the pool and gone back in. Let them.

Action items:

- Let the jets cool first. Come back to the conversation when things settle down—you both need a moment.
- Remember that your child, while insane right now, is learning things about life. Let them learn about themselves.
- Let yourself off the hook if you make a mistake, you may make a few. Just learn from them and get better.
- Get SO good at not reacting to any past or current hormonal eruptions that they only have themselves to blame.

Key point here… do NOT say or do anything that could be used against you. You lose your cool, and the fight turns to what you did and not what they did. An old lesson we learned from the scorpions! (See "I Forgive You, You Psycho!")

Remember, you can't fix this, you can only hope to survive it!

Step 11

SET BOUNDARIES.

Balance freedom with responsibility. They need guidance and structure, even if they don't always admit it.

I Love You, **YOU LITTLE SH!T**

The goal at this point:

Give that little devil enough rope to swing, but not enough to hang herself.

The stuff you still have control over includes:

- Your house, your rules
- Treating you and others with respect
- Reminding them that you love them (despite their awful, shitty, fucked up treatment of you)
- Allow certain things to pass so your little devil knows when things are serous enough for you to bring the hammer down!

Step 12

CELEBRATE SMALL VICTORIES AND IMAGINE A FUTURE WHERE THEY COME BACK TO YOU—BECAUSE THEY WILL.

Remember to take a moment and celebrate every small win; every time they smile, give you a hug, or thank you for something.

And celebrate yourself every day. You're a fucking god. Surviving teenage girls is a superhuman feat!

Go out and buy that cape you've been eyeing. You deserve it!

Meditate on the following every morning before the shit storm:

- They were once your glowing angel, don't forget that.
- Being a teenage nightmare is normal and hard for them—remember, they've never known anything beyond this point.
- There will come a day when you wish that little asshole was around so you could be annoyed by her.
- She will grow up, go away, and have her own life.
- She will—hopefully—provide you with grandchildren.
- She will—hopefully—be there when you pass, loving you, honoring you, mourning you and remembering your heart, your courage, and your dedication.

KAT AND STEWART'S FINAL THOUGHTS:

- All of this is normal.
- You're a good parent.
- You're not going to get paid back or win an award.
- You're going to hate them for a while.
- And then it will be over before you know it.
- You're doing your best, and each day is going to be different, so flexibility under chaos is paramount.

It's hard to imagine getting through this time. It seems like the lovely little baby you watched grow to a little princess is auditioning for Exorcist V. Where did my little girl go? She went to the next logical place in her life—and remember, this is HER life we're talking about.

The point of this book is to remind you how great you are for even attempting the feat of raising a daughter. But if you did it right, and there is no right way to do it, you're going to end up with a well-adjusted woman who makes you forget all about that little shit that hijacked you all those years ago.

DEFINITION OF TERMS

Puberty
[PEW • burr-dee]

That awkward, hideously bizarre stage in life where you go through the most dramatic change you could imagine other than dying. For boys, it means weird smells, a disgusting room, and some beanpole taller than you. For girls, it's more complex. Girls see this oncoming change as a window into womanhood, and they prepare for it the moment it starts—which means no more little girl, so fuck off parents!

Hormones
[Horr • moe-ns]

Little bullets of shitty, fuck-you energy that course through a teen's bloodstream, rendering them completely devoid of rational, empathetic thoughts.

Sarcasm
[SAHR-kå-zim]

A teenager's best weapon of defense when confronted with the following: truth; kindness; reality; a favor; a request; a ride; a meal; a thought; an idea; your breathing (see dictionary for all other scenarios—start with A).

www.ingramcontent.com/pod-product-compliance
Lightning Source LLC
Chambersburg PA
CBHW051617010526
44119CB00008B/187